AS A TEEN
WHERE DO YOU STAND
WITH CHRIST?

VERENA SMITH

authorHOUSE®

AuthorHouse™
1663 Liberty Drive
Bloomington, IN 47403
www.authorhouse.com
Phone: 1 (800) 839-8640

Published by AuthorHouse 06/10/2020

ISBN: 978-1-7283-6446-9 (sc)
ISBN: 978-1-7283-6445-2 (e)

CONTENTS

CHAPTER ONE

TEEN STRUGGLES

As a teen, you go through many struggles such as Depression, Bullying, Drugs, Peer pressure, and social media.

Depression

Depression can be and is very tough on a person let alone a teen. You may feel as if you are all alone and there is nobody here to help you. The good news is that the Lord Jesus Christ will never leave you. When you feel as if you are alone, call up to him. He will listen to everything you have to say. He will not judge you but he will help you get through any situation. God has many verses in the bible where he is explaining how he will NEVER leave you. When reading Isaiah 41:10, KJV he says that "Fear thou not; for I am with thee: be not dismayed; for I am thy God: I will strengthen thee; yea, I will help thee; yea, I will uphold thee with the right hand of my righteousness." With that being said you are never alone in this world. The Lord Jesus Christ will never leave your side. He's the one you can call your friend, Best friend and even family. As a teen you have been a prisoner to lies and to all deception of the enemy, you have been deep down in a hole covered with depression and anxiety. The Lord Jesus wants to set you free from depression. In order for Jesus to set you free, you must believe in him that he is the son of God. "For God so loved the world, that he gave his only begotten Son, that whosoever believeth in him should not perish, but have everlasting life." (John 3:16, KJV)

Bullying

Bullying is something that can bring you down. A lot of people get made fun of for being poor or smelling bad. But God said that "Thou shalt not avenge, nor bear any grudge against the children of thy people, but thou shalt love thy neighbour as thyself: I am the LORD." (Lev 19:18, KJV). With that being said God didn't put us on this earth to be judged, we were put here to love each other no matter what. Nobody should feel down because they don't have everything, everything down here is going to be temporary. It is never about the money, it's about the faith you have in Christ.

Drugs

Drugs are very dangerous. They can mess with your mind and make you go on the wrong road. I as a teen has had a good share of experimenting with drugs. Do I wish I could take it back? Yes I do, let me tell you why. When I was doing drugs I didn't feel like myself. I felt as if I had to hide everything I was doing, it was very confusing. I got addicted and started doing stupid stuff. I am telling you all of this so you don't end up like, I want you to know its help on the way. God once said that "No temptation has overtaken you except what is common to mankind. And God is faithful; he will not let you be tempted beyond what you can bear. But when you are tempted, he will also provide a way out so that you can endure it." Even if you do find yourself in the wrong place there is help to get you out of that situation. You don't have to feel as if you are stuck in this prison. Christ Jesus wants you to know that you shouldn't keep quiet if there is something that doesn't feel right then say something. There will forever be hope for you, all you have to do is call upon the one who sits up high.

Peer pressure

Peer pressure is an act that can lead teens to participate in actions that can lead them to go down the wrong path. Some teens feel as if they don't go on with the actions they won't fit in. I personally have never experienced peer pressure but I have seen what it has done with my child. Her coming home from school acting different and wanting to act like people in her school while she is only in elementary school gets me wondering. If she is only eight years old going through this then what are teens going through. God didn't put us on this earth to be like anybody down here or to try to listen to men. In Acts 5:29, KJV he says, "Then Peter and the other apostles answered and said, We ought to obey God rather than men." That means he will deliver you from any of your trouble, nothing is too big for God. You have to obey God and not men because he is the one who sent his Son from heaven to die on the cross for our sins. God is the one who created heaven and earth. Men didn't come out of their way to make sure you are saved, ask yourself is it really worth it. Is it worth going to hell just to please men? NO it's not, eternal heaven sounds better than eternal burning. Jesus Christ said in John 14:6, KJV "Jesus saith unto him, I am the way, the truth, and the life: no man cometh unto the Father, but by me." That means you can only have life through Jesus. Jesus is the only one who can save lives. Men can't help you go to heaven but they, sure enough, can make you go to hell. "And these shall go away into everlasting punishment: but the righteous into life eternal." (Matthew 25:46, KJV)

Social Media

Growing up I never had technology so I didn't really understand the concept of any type of social media. Over the years the way I have seen the way the internet has developed and I can truly say it's dangerous. My teen daughter has social media and it really shocked me on how somebody can know where you are in a click of a button. The Lord Jesus Christ doesn't want you to invest all of your time in something that won't help you go to heaven.

John 15:10, KJV Jesus Christ says "If ye keep my commandments, ye shall abide in my love; even as I have kept my Father's commandments, and abide in his love." This means instead of loving something that has no life you should keep your mind on Jesus and not the things of this world.

CHAPTER TWO

FORGIVENESS

A lot of people have a hard time forgiving. This can and will lead you to hell if you don't repent. Why not forgive the person then hold a grudge and go to hell. No matter what you have done once you have asked God to forgive you he will. If reading James 5:16, KJV, "Confess your faults one to another, and pray one for another, that ye may be healed. The effectual fervent prayer of a righteous man availeth much." When you repent it helps you live happier. Forgiveness is a thing that won't let you feel guilty. Forgiveness is about letting go of your past and not having a heavy heart. If you call yourself a Christian and is not willing to forgive then your blessings might set back. You have to really sit down and have a conversation with god because if you don't, it will be really difficult. With all the temptations in this world, it is going to be hard. Some people use the term "Forgive and Forget." I'm here to tell you that there is no such thing written in the bible. You must forgive the ones who hurt you. As teens, you may get in an argument with one of your friends and think "I will never forgive them for what they have done." The feeling of betrayal is really hard to deal with. Forgive your friend and put it behind you. In the bible when Judas betrayed Jesus, Jesus forgave him. God didn't make us think badly about each other, but to uplift each other. "And be ye kind one to another, tenderhearted, forgiving one another, even as God for Christ's sake hath forgiven you." (Ephesians 4:32, KJV). We all have made mistakes that have made God upset with us or even sad, maybe talking bad about one of your classmates, teachers, and maybe even the principal. Do you think this was pleasing in God's eyes?

CHAPTER THREE

WHO IS YOUR GOD?

In John 3:16, KJV Jesus said, "For God so loved the world, that he gave his only begotten Son, that whosoever believeth in him should not perish, but have everlasting life." In order for you to have everlasting, you must believe that Jesus is the son of god, so you won't perish. Jesus came to restore lives that means Jesus is GOD Himself. In John 14:6, KJV "Jesus saith unto him, I am the way, the truth, and the life: no man cometh unto the Father, but by me." Lives only comes through Jesus Christ, and no one else. You been to the discos, clubs, and parties, but you have never found satisfaction. Jesus Christ came to be your God, he came to give you comfort, he came to give you satisfaction, and he came to heal your broken heart. As a teen are you ready for Jesus to be your God? Are you ready to put the world behind and put God first? by you putting Jesus Christ first place in your life .you have made the right choice, even friend may neglect, the Lord Jesus will never forsake you. "Be strong and of a good courage, fear not, nor be afraid of them: for the LORD thy God, he it is that doth go with thee; he will not fail thee, nor forsake thee." (Deuteronomy 31:6, KJV). You have to choose a God to serve the God of this world or Jesus Christ which came to save the world from being lost. Luke 9:56, KJV "For the Son of man is not come to destroy men's lives, but to save them. And they went to another village." That means Jesus Christ only in the business of saving lives. As a teen do you want to be saved? Or do you want to experience life with Jesus as Lord and savior of your life? You must believe in Him that he is the son of God. You must choose between the two. And be certain of whom you believe in. Christ said In Luke 16:13, KJV "No servant can serve two masters: for either he will hate the one, and love the other; or else he will hold to the one, and despise the other. Ye cannot serve God and mammon." As I said before choose between the two. You have a choice to choose God or the devil. But do you know the choice that you make in this life determines the decision of your destination. Either eternal life with Jesus in heaven, or eternal hell with satan the devil. As a teen if you just happily gave your life to Jesus Christ. As you go through life with Jesus Christ. You may experience lots of difficulty with friends and family and temptation will come in your way. Be aware of it and be strong in the Lord and in the power of His might. Even friends you may know they may say things to trouble your heart because you have left the World Behind and you have to put Jesus first place in your life. Besides all of this, always trust in the Lord that he will fight your battles for you. Have faith in God in Jesus name. Jesus Christ said in John 14:1, KJV "Let not your heart be troubled: ye believe in God, believe also in me." Have faith in God that Jesus Christ is real and He is God. And I was in newborn Christian you need a friend in Christ Jesus that will be there for you. life with Christ Jesus it's not an easy Road but Trust in the Lord that he will take care of you and he will also carry your burden John 14:18, KJV "I will not leave you comfortless: I will come to you. "That means he is always with you. John 14:18, ESV "I will not leave you as orphans; I will come to you".

CHAPTER FOUR

OBEDIENCE

A s a teen sometimes you get upset when your parents tell you that you can't do some things that you wanted to do. Maybe you wanted to go to that party across town but your parents said no but you sneak out any way that's very disappointing in God's eye. God wants us to obey our parents no matter what the problem is. In 1 John 2:17, ESV it says "And the world is passing away along with its desires, but whoever does the will of God abides forever". This means that all of the things you see such as the money, cars, and businesses are only here temporary, but whoever obeys God, will live with him forever. I teach all my kids that it is very important to obey me because in Ephesians 6:1, ESV it states that" Children, obey your parents in the Lord, for this is right. Children obey your parents in the Lord for it is right to honor your father and mother. This is the first commandment with promised and long life. He will add to you that means you must obey God to receive everlasting life because life only comes through Jesus Christ and no one else so if you want Everlasting life you must obey the word that Jesus Christ spoke of God. As childrens if you obey the word of God you will grow into his love and experience his presence. As you obey the word of God and continue to love of God you will have the strength of Jesus Christ to let go of the pain and the hatred of unforgiveness. Now you will have the power of Christ to forgive. If you do not feel like doing it, remember 2 Corinthians 5:7, ESV "for we walk by faith, not by sight" this means that you must obey by the word of God and not the things you see with your eyes that is passing away. Jesus Christ said In Matthew 5:18, KJV . For verily I say unto you, Till heaven and earth pass, one jot or one tittle shall in no wise pass from the law, till all be fulfilled. You must leave by the word of God in Jesus name amen. As a teen, you end up meeting new friends in life and sometimes they want to direct your stamp advising you of things to do when you are ready to know the word of God. And you already know better the word of God which sets your path straight. And even say things like it's okay if you go out or disobey your parents and have you turning away from the faith of

God. Are you going to obey Satan that is working through them trying to take you to hell as he tried to destroy the foundation of the word of God in you? By deception and lies. Satan promises you the world and the things of the world. Or are you going to obey the word of God Jesus Christ spokes of God and the truth of God and the things of God? life only comes through Jesus Jesus Christ promises us everlasting life joy and happiness and laughter. Satan promises you the world you do not need the world you already have the world with you. You need Jesus Christ to help you obey God's word and Jesus Christ is working through the. Holy Spirit of God in you. As he guides you into all truth of God all you have to do is to obey God's word and you shall have everlasting life in Jesus name. So everlasting life only comes through Christ. If you want everlasting life you have to come to. The Lord Jesus. Now the principle of God is to be obedient to God's word. as we live in this world. you know this is the world is an unfair world lots of trouble and. Pain caused by, others. But they really don't care about the situation. When someone gets hurt, it's by another man fault. Besides all of this, you must forgive the ones who hurt, to obey Gods word. So the word of God is fulfilled in your heart. So that means that the word of God has a place in your heart so that you are willing to always forgive another. So that the love of God could live among us as teens.

CHAPTER FIVE

THE LOVE OF GOD

J esus said in John 15:12, ESV "This is my commandment, that you love one another as I have loved you". The commandment of Jesus Christ is to love one another. We have to remain in His words to keep His love and to do what He says to do. Strength in one another in trials and bearing with each other comforting one another in the word of the Lord Jesus. With the same words of comfort that the Lord comforted us. That we may also love one another as He loved us. And this is why we keep Christ commandment. Love is a very powerful and strong word. Jesus Christ came down from heaven on Earth to teach us of God's Love. In addition, show us how to love one another. Us people hurt other people's feelings but in order for Gods love to continue living in us we must let go of the old man's deeds. You may say how we go about doing this we must remain in the Commandment of Jesus. That we love one another as he loved us. As teens, we go through the pain with each other bearing the burden of each other in Christ Jesus. Hard time a good time with each other. Trust in the Lord Jesus. Philippians 4:13, KJV "I can do all things through Christ which strengtheneth me". The Lord is our strength. God has shown us love in so many ways man have not. He has forgiven us for things that are bad. He loves us even when we do wrong. We should love each other just like God loves us. God didn't make us hate each other and fight against each other but love each other like brother and sister in Christ. People may offend you at work at home or even among your family members but why should you hold a grudge against them or let that stand in your way. Instead of alluding yourself to respond to God's love in a very humble way. Forgiving those who trespass against you or hurt you and those who say things to hurt you. Simple things people could say and it May hurt you. Not even knowing how the enemy approach so quickly. In a very discouraging way we don't have to rely upon and the words of the enemy. However, in Jesus name, we must always willing to forgive one another. That the love of God may continue living in. Our hearts. No matter what the situation may be how horrible out of it lets continue living in the love of Christ that we may go to heaven with Jesus Christ and live with him in heaven. Jesus already said we must love one another as He loved us and this is his commandment. It is to love one another. John Chapter 14: 2-3, KJV "In my Father's house are many mansions: if it were not so, I would have told you. I go to prepare a place for you. And if I go and prepare a place for you, I will come again, and receive you unto myself; that where I am, there ye may be also." That means he is coming back with us to go to heaven with him as we continue in his love. Because there is no love in this world and truth but only hate. That is why Jesus Christ came to teaches us Of God's Love and his truth that we may live in it. You must always make a Time for God in your heart. In Jesus name spending time with him praying fasting that, you may continue in his love. Pray always. Jesus laid his life down for us. He gave his life for us and he died on the cross for us on Calvary to save our Life from being Parish. He shared his blood for our sin that he washes our sins in his own blood and that is how much he loves us. He gave his life to bring us back to the father God the Father he had to give something to receive us in return and that is his life. And that's how much he loves us and that's why it's written John 3:16, KJV "For God so loved the world, that he gave his only begotten Son, that whosoever believeth in him should not perish, but have everlasting life." If you accept the son of God you accept God's love. The love of God brings peace.

My name is. Verena Smith, I hope you enjoy this book and hope it will help you that you may believe in Jesus Christ that he's all about saving lives. The lives of the lost sheep of God that they may be found in the son of God.

John 3:16, KJV" "For God so loved the world, that he gave his only begotten Son, that whosoever believeth in him should not perish, but have everlasting life."

||| ||| |█ || █|||█ | █ ██| |.|█ ||█   ██| ██ | | ███|| | |█ █ ██|